Oh, for Nothing

Jesse R. Bodley

Table of Contents

Lacey Girl 1

One Euthanization..2

Lucky Dogs...3

To Never Wake Up 4

Bullet Points...5

Failed Bohemians.......................................6

Existential Conclusions 7

The Sepulchral Ruins.................................8

Change 10

Conniption Fit..12

Perception 13

If Not For Her 14

Breathless Song 15

Alone In Winter.......................................16

Only Now We See.....................................17

Security..18

Arc 19

Always A Remainder 20

Why Do I Do This To Myself 21

Smile Insanity 22

Failure In Life 23

Sunset Deicide 24

Transmigration Of Souls........................25

Relapse 26

Left 27

Predestination 28

Adieu 29

The Good Wolf 30

Sewing Room 31

Isolation And Alienation 32

A Summertime Dream 33

Plaster Of Paris 35

Karmic Cruelty 36

Mirror Monster 38

Low And Limerent 39

Can't Rely 40

Death Rattles 41

LSD Day 42

Elegance 43

If You're There 44

The Gods Are Unconcerned 46

All The World Lost 47

Complex 49

Who Am I Kidding 51

Babble 52

Anathema 53

Insecurity 54

Delusions 55

Renewal 56

Things Which Do Not Matter..57

Best To Have A Friend 59

Regret 60

Personal History..61

This Thing Is Understanding...62

Freeform 63

Mayday 64

Vulnerable 65

Routine Digression...66

Hair Trigger..67

Bummer..68

Note...69

Depression 70

When I'm Dying..72

Sadnesses..73

Satellite Sunlight...74

The Real Me 75

Lost Face..76

Now, Then...77

Corpses And Dinners...78

The Miscarriage That Is My Life 79

Whatever 80

Strange Bird 81

The Cold Is Warm...82

Beyond Origin 83

The Only Thing Worse Than Poetry......................................84

I Don't Get To Be A Person 85

Cliche 86

Make Your Bed And Lie In It...87

The Very Same..88

Anomie 89

Lacey Girl

As a child, I was free only among the trees, where I
walked a wooded trail—in chase of my dog's tail.

She led as she wagged and waited if I lagged—behind,
to heel beside me with the patience of a lab.

I'd heed her front paw lift up and point with her nose
as she straightened her tail—and listened for the danger

which waited round the trail. 'Til she was sure, as nature
is so pure, our souls should continue—sail our bodies

down the trail. Across gated pastures where cattle grazed,
to meadows, swamps, and a creek of sweet water, where

we were raised. There in the meadows, we would smell
and pick the flowers—to take with us to the swamp, and

drop as we would count the hours. And by and by, we ran
along the creek—so high, and a current raged below the

surface, which reflected not only the blue sky, but a boy
and his dog, who both could fly.

One Euthanization

How old you are, now
—and still I see a pup.
How gray you are; a
last sip you take, from

the supple cup. Now, so
feeble, decrepit and senile.
I remember you, then,
teething on my shoe laces,

my Lacey Girl. Darlin', we
were children together, crated
in our indifference to the world.
I saw you read my unspoken

words. You heeled to my side;
you felt my dirge. We went for
a ride; I felt us merge. Our heart
is a tide; our soul is a surge.

Lucky Dogs

It must be better not to know;
there is nowhere to go.
It does not matter either way,
whether I lie around all day,
or I put on another show,
there's just nowhere to go.
Listen to their words,
spoken before the thought,
baying in the night light,
not wondering in poor sight.
They are better in their way,
just run around and play all day.

To Never Wake Up

How safe and sound is the ground;
can I drown in her nightgown?
Never again want to go to town.
Oh, put me deep in the earth,
a mound in the ground,
asleep nice 'n sound.
Digging a hole and closing my eyes,
going nowhere—there everything dies,
dreaming no sweet dreams—telling no lies.
Oh, how safe and sound is the ground?
Stay tucked away. No, you may
never visit, everybody go away.
Please, commit my remains;
deliver the insane from the rain,
of all earthly pleasure and pain.
Oh, please be there only darkness after,
close my eyes forever,'cause there's nothing
to see here—and no reason to be here.

Bullet Points

- I'm always becoming worse than I've been,
- just one more day, then more days ahead.
- Something's intruding and has always been,
- I am nothing's twin—from nowhere, then.
- We have all we need to start again,
- no one's seed—nothing, I can't grow them
- because we're all coming apart from within.
- Just one more day, then more days ahead.
- Here's one so forthcoming—shot right
- through my head.

Failed Bohemians

Be cautious of the man who knows
not what to do, for he may do anything.
Be wary of the strange and weird,
and the—never meant for this world,
for they will fall.

The worse it ever becomes, the better
it ever may be. Just listen to the music,
heard from the smokey dinges, where
derelicts become enlightened—and
want to bring you there,

compelling, seducing—becoming the clay
from which you were molded, encompassing,
possessing, demanding attention to the human
spirit. And fall prey to one's own demon, who
glides on a riff of determination, and proudly

perches upon prospect. To perceive, conceive, and
devise an ending conclusion of the sort, as madness
begets madness. And never knowing, still feel—
compelled by a wonderful fortune—that here and now
you still stand—alive and well even when they fell.

Existential Conclusions

My friend, if you have to ask, and can't recall
what is lost—then, surely I cannot help you.

My friend, accept my consolation, the world
is a playground—full of rides and slides, and

everyone is playing. Some swing from bars
and chains, while others spin the merry go

round, but there are those very few in the
recesses of childhood, still inside the turtle's

sandbox; and their toys are ravaged fossils
of origins vast and forgotten, and no sooner

do they reach in, than they discover their own
attention, and forget to dig the golden desert.

My friend, do not despair. Tell me, why should
we not play the game; why not better just to play

along, when all the world feels the same, as that
which is lost and all gone, and once and for all

has said goodbye—and by and by, has chosen a lie?
And by the bye, from how to why, has chosen to die.

The Sepulchral Ruins

It's not easy to realize—that what's right is all that you
despise. Searching with these eyes, all these eyes have
seen so keenly, have been lies. And to feel like you've
wasted your life in some undeniable, existential strife.

That there's so much pain in this life, too much to wane
before the next life. And to know it hurts just to keep
you awake, in some still and stagnant, impure,
unparalleled lake. That there's nothing in the wake
of your splashing, your thrashing, or your sake.

Left to analyze your own demise, all alone with no
faith to immortalize the hope that reflects in your eyes
—those eyes are going blind.

It's not hard to recognize, all that matters is in her eyes,
when she's searching for her reflection in your guise,
casting a lure of affection to your mise, hooking onto
the surprise in your eyes. And you feel like you're
wasting your time, delayed in the haste you've made.

That for too long you've laid in your grave, forever to wade this charade. And to know the pain of too late, so little time but you just had to wait. That too late is your fate, and your heart is the bait, hooked by reverie, and reeled by hate.

Left to analyze your own demise, all alone with no faith to immortalize, the hope that reflects in your eyes —those eyes are going blind.

Change

Make an impression, (any will do.)
Make known your presence; act a fool.
Smile more often and laugh all the time.
Let out the anger, and let in a stranger.

Funny now, (and curious how—when
your best efforts amount to nothing,)
impulse glides in on a whim to amuse
your nature. That deeply suppressed,

insolent nature, known from time to time,
though, rarely seen and often stricken
from thought—ought not be confused,
(it was after all) the pain we sought.

From boredom born of mid-December,
and reminisced through photographs,
fading to remember—June is lost
to mid-year timber.

Drinking, eating, meeting with existence—
all the little pleasures and all the resistance.
Is there one question asked not with persistence?
Is there one answer? Is there—one answer

to a question with some subsistence,
(let alone of substance?) Dispose of that which
we've dropped on the floor, drinking too much
too fast, giving up the future to forget the past.

Deeper the dive, the more shallow the pool.
Have I no blood or am I a fool? Is there not loss
in temperaments—cool? Watch out, here I go
—am I a tool? As I have learned more of humanity

in an hour of repression, than those who
in a lifetime of promiscuity could quicken
their spirits, or for in that hour, that forever
winding, whining hour of self-hate—I felt

only an eternity of longing to release.
To fill indefinitely this unnatural mind,
(the only space in time, not made up in kind.)
To unearth this mortal tomb with a loud

and a deafening boom. No, rest assured,
I am still here. A lonely poet finding meaning
in the lowly things I do. I seek it out,
and make of it what I will.

Conniption Fit

Ah, this murderous madness.
Oh, this suicidal sadness.

This great irreparable damage that
sings to my defeat, from somewhere

deep inside the molecular maelstrom
—from somewhere far and wide,

stretched beside the winding—whining
of my mind.

Ah, yes—this memorable mistress.
Oh, this seductive sadist.

These grand and irreversible coercions
which triumph with deceit,

over something seeped inside, some
—thing crept and seeped within

to this cellular design.
To chain with indecision to a wall

of inhibition—while barred from life
in a dungeon of conniption.

Perception

Imagination pulls on non-essence
as masturbation gives my heart
away—to strangers (none other
than pleasantry, embroidered by
passion, and woven by quaint and
only friends delighted by flattery.)

A tapestry of unfair color and intrigue,
shadowed by modesty and illusion,
drawn together with contrast by disarray
and complemented by its own seclusion,
from those who, in their own self-serving
infamy, forever drew a veil—swung open,
a curtain to blind that which is sought
and not found, (sought to find a window
to their own avail.) A blind pulled and

dropped, (allowed to drop and not caught,)
by the open heart of sunlight and too—
the dark, which forever swung the day
in a deep, salty, pastel sea—which fraught
forever, is a life that wills to be, and still,
that sea blue eye does not see.

If Not For Her

Why it means so much, I—don't know if I
even know how. Should I let it go, now—
that everything is lost, and how—have I
made it through and shall—I go on
without this galle?

Always aware of snakes in the grass.
Still, it has not come to pass. All I need
are reasons why, and still in mind—will
not die. There she goes, skips around—
across my fate, striking, sparking,
igniting my hate.

The flame, does it burn down? It leaves
its embers to smolder—and wind blows
in from another, over my shoulder.

Why, I do not look around? Why, I do not
turn around? If not to hold her, if not to
love her—that cool breeze blown over
—my shoulder just gets colder.

Breathless Song

Why do I sing—bring this nothing song of mine,
to spring or silence. One or the other, I can either
keep my visions to myself and die inside, alone
and silent—with another by my side, or scream
the violence and waste the world, that rapturous
violet. Why I sing and sing, this thing of mine,
this gift I've been given. This is love? It's not
love that I'm feeling. It's this nothing, no love,
breathless—song I'm still singing.

Alone In Winter

Walking on snow is like chewing chocolate. First, the two compact and then crush outward, one beneath my bootheels, the other between my molars. Both so equally exciting: one so warmly; the other so coldly inviting.

The senses like to dance with emotion, to come together, entangle, become one. Love to perpetuate, forever a single moment, as when all things pure inevitably dissolve.

Becoming a solution from its most basic essence, to take up form in the likeness of a feeling, one of conclusion and confidence of its own resolve (however, obsessive-compulsive.) That effect itself is a cause, one of irreconcilable indifference, that never will yearn but always crave, (to a degree the world can only wonder) eternal winter in an act of redress.

Only Now We See

Ah, a child, and how very adorable. And why should it not be? It is, after all, (it does, after all—belong to none other.) How very proud you are, indeed. And why should you not be? You are, after all, who sacrifices all, the little fledgling infant's mother, or father. And you wish to reflect your love, to cast an image of affection upon your love, and be kind in love, and be loved. And so you raise with care, your most cherished of all; you do not dare—expose them to a world not beside—you, will not share. And you keep them close, kenneled up beside you, (that they never chose) never to expound even when they rose, forever there beside you (ever so close.) And so now you see, (ever so clearly) only now you see. You raised not a person but a companion, see. Your children have a future, see? (Despite your past) But not as your pets, and if you continue treat and raise them like animals, they will break free from all restraint, and turn on you as such.

Security

Digging through a hamper, waste baskets turned up.
Searching for an answer, but a waxed paper cup.
Kicking pebbles in the street. How far will they go,
strolling along the beat, with nowhere to go?
Standing post at the gate, how long will he wait?
Opening for no one—the sentry is one, all alone
in the world. Behind a door, is a creature of solitude.
When will she knock; or will she beat it down?
How long will she stay? When she leaves she forgets
to secure its place. Now, there is nothing between man
and beast: one will search for answers; one will feast.

Arc

There is my home off in the distance;
I see this place with my own eyes.
There is nothing in between us, now;
it is so clear, up here—so high.

I roamed alone, I scaled a mountain;
I was lost, I had no guide.
I only followed that intense heat,
however cold, however numb.

And when I felt the cold wind blow,
I heard the trees applauding.
For as I tracked barefoot through snow,
only then—I found my calling.

Always A Remainder

They were all so right.
They, who said—I am not like they are.
That is correct. Now, I remember those days.
Early in the morning and as the sun was rising,
I was still sleeping.
Marked me as tardy, or better yet, absent still.
Teacher made me play catch up against my will.
Then, I could hear them laughing, my class-
mates, my peers—when my back was turned,
I was facing the chalkboard,
working out the problems they gave me.
I was no volunteer. They made me, oh
—how I found a solution.
I turned around, and I turned around.
I stood there spinning circles as the
eternal remainder.
Heard someone say, "what's his problem?"
Now, I did not answer, and neither did
anyone else, and as I spun beyond
all control, I could hear no laughter.

Why Do I Do This To Myself

My Grandfather was a drunk, (no point here.)
My uncle was a drunkard, I'm just here.

I remember a time when we were on our way to the county fair,
and my uncle was in the back seat; he found a bottle of liquor
and went to town, and by the time we got there and all of a sudden,
he was a lot like my grandfather, and my mother was there too.

I inquired where the bottle had come from. My mother answered,
(because he was supposed to be on the wagon,) that the van
belonged to a great uncle, (who was a gambler—and
a degenerate, and a drunk, and a trucker.)

And while we were there we enjoyed our uncle's company, so.
He was a great guy; he played the guitar and was a lover and, oh
—how many women loved him, and how I wanted to be just like him
when I grew up, but when I grew up I had to realize that I
wasn't at all like my uncle or my grandfather in any way
except that I'm a drunk.

I wish that I was loved by women, but it seems the bottle only cares.
And who cares about pathetic drunks or depressed poets or mothers?
And who cares about dead drunk grandfathers and uncles and fares?
Who cares about regrets that aren't theirs?

Smile Insanity

She called me Smiley. (That's right, Smiley.)
Sort of like you'd call a large man Tinie.

'Cause I never smiled, I never smiled.
Had every reason to, yeah, but never did.

And then, she met a guy, and he said, hi. Yeah,
and he smiled wide, and that is why,

I am all alone, no one to hold,
no one to hold me, yeah, it's just me.

Oh, can't you see that it's defeated me?
Why can't I see? Oh, it's killing me.

Is it a sin that I turned in?
I turned in—now, lately, I grin.

Where could she be, that one like the sea?
Where could she be? If she could see me,

and oh, how I'm smiling. No reason to,
but it's smile or die, even though I'm so shy.

Failure In Life

Just one more point of view,
as to what I'm doing wrong.
(What you ought to do)
—I've heard this song.
Something empty
desperately needs a filling.
Dust fan cloud a 'spinning,
makes a face on my ceiling.
Look, smoke—done filled the room.
Wait, better not to assume.
Knock on the door, and whom
—hits that black plume?
And they look away,
they all just turn away.
Suppose it's better to breathe
than to tear up and suffocate.

Sunset Deicide

In a moment, and at any given time I am at a loss,
for time has only told (with whispered rumors in the cold)
—of an opportunity lost.

What vigilance has persisted without correction?
What mind will discipline without the lesson?
One has to find a way without direction.

And so looks back with wonder where it comes from.
There lies a mossy stone on which to rest,
and dreams in deep sleep do not move on.

Can't undo what has been done,
cannot raise—the setting sun.

Transmigration Of Souls

Alone, revisiting old ghosts—his demons wait patiently.
The woods, a solitary sanctuary, instinctually void of question.
A silence there, warding off all supposed good with all its
dumbfounded fellowship. Herein, but neither beside—nor above
or below in otherworldly realms, but within his own existing
consciousness, stands without reason or purpose, but only with
a knowledge, clean and clear, as only demise can ever be,
lays his head upon the Earth, and looks up to find heaven
in a confession—that nothing he sees.

Relapse

No sobriety within me,
no true colors I can't see.
No love for the sadly whimsy,
no release for the empty.
Taken to the shadows—let fall,
the pillars of society.
Given to the dead end—force all,
through the door insanity.
Sober now and reckoning—I see,
one true face of humanity.

Left

Pushing me forward through this door,
revolving, not knowing what's in store.
Following the lead, only wanting more,
contesting doubt with an unfair score.
Threshold broken and I step out door,
look up to sky—where the avian soar.
Regress and withdraw, whatever for?
To see and long—the one I adore.
To stroll alone in thought, to bore
—to toss aside a seedless core,
as bird of prey, above and fore
circle 'round as hunger for,
what lingers on as fall to floor
—peck away all things in store.

Predestination

I reached adulthood slow, as a child cannot know,
though, in the day of a lovely spring—felt only lonely,
one solitary thing.

Not caressed by newborn earth, but put to rest
not long after birth.

And when a thousand tears, a thought could vanquish,
still not a prayer could square the anguish—as divine
concept could never seem—with vision and wonder,

that of a dream

But as fear and detriment, despite the infinite possibility,
for the cold, gray, winter's sting, of the
never may tone—predestiny.

Adieu

I brushed with midnight blue and thought it must be true,
bland white canvas with no hue, and so I painted it for you.

So much is there ado, and with nothing much to do,
I delved deep into the blue. True, it was for myself that I drew,
but only because of you that I knew it to be true
—when the olden is then new, and the fallen up and flew
—closer, yet further from you, far from color, far from blue.

In order to never misconstrue, my moonlight white—from your
midnight blue, but I leave you one thing true, as one became
from two.

Alone forever, though I am too—so very much in love with you,
and alone, this is the dowry—that I've refused for you.

The Good Wolf

Take her torn lingerie—or lie down beside, to be loyal and honest,
though, not by nature—but by choice of virtue.

A wolf born not of the wild but from the kennel, battles with inherent
instinct, neither sheep nor sheepdog—rather, ravenous, bloodthirsty
fiend wrapped in wool cloth—persuaded gently with docility
commanded, not to hunt but to wait patiently, to heel and walk
by a length of rope.

To feed but not devour, still, he watches with cunning and listens,
bravely detects a cold undertone of cruel and vehement provocation.
Kicked out by sheep, bit down by sheepdog. So, longs for the morale,
to run the pack—coven, with bearing teeth, to growl, to snarl, to howl
at the moon.

Track and sniff out her perfume, the deer, the rabbit, the sheep;
and tear the flesh—and hide, and let spill the blood, yet too soft
for the pack, too predatory for the herd. Must escape or wait—
to be slid the sloshing bowl. Why the wolf, so mistreated, thus—
still bears a noble soul.

Sewing Room

Oh, please dear elder have not forgotten,
a day long since—past as one lost button.
Would that thread and needle forever hem,
mean be tattered and torn at seam?
Could that, the ancestral spirit still linger on
as moth, which stir outside the linen cabinet?
Has not your gown since fallen down long ago,
from shrunken form and wrinkled skin,
still lustrous in its fervor? Ah, perfume
—laced in silken lingerie with feline grace.
Which is it, only phase with tussling yarn,
or spun the living organ with heavy garments?
How is it gone, all elegance with the sensual;
or wrung from hands a touch of wonton?
Whereby, to dusty ramshackled rooms,
somewhere warm and dim can welcome
the company of lovers into bed?

Isolation And Alienation

Dug a hole deep in the—ground, so many thoughts,
although, no sound. Only this I have found, within

the earth, heaven and hell impound. And it is so very
clear, spring will soon be here, to recycle rot or embellish

—fear forgotten, all but taste—love in cold cheap beer.
Skinned scalp and hide, polished leather—I never.

Imposters, cold and clever—blame it on the weather.
How long now, I'm alone? Gone into another zone.

Buried over the flesh and bone, collect my skeletal clone,
with hair and nails so long—you'll cut yourself.

What has gone wrong? Just sing and dance all night long.
So dark and silent, don't fool yourself—this is not wrong.

A Summertime Dream

Some nobody lies down in his bed, cradled in his own
acquired filth, sometime during the day's high noon
to rest before rising for the third shift.

He watches the ceiling fan spinning particles of dust
through half-closed eyes—the light past an open window
envisions the universe and falls in.

To sleep he wanders down a hallway, naked flesh knocking
on shut doors of vacant rooms with low ceilings, recently
abandoned by poor tenants.

A shudder, dust-stained dry walls and silhouettes of old, dingy
furniture, and dry rotted floors—carpeted blue, strewn
with food crumbs and bits of torn old newspaper wrappings,
moldering beneath abandonment.

Moving on with air-chilled bones down moaning stairways,
reaching up from distant foyers, welcoming descent, yet
offering escape—parallel to basement-level entrances
of incomprehensible dark.

He hears the singing of birds, just outside through paned
side door windows, and can see their bath and feel their
seed on the bottoms of his offal-covered and tired feet.

Oh, if not for their pause at his attention, he might not
step back, or fall away with yielding hinges, into empty
dark matter, sweat-soaked bed sheets
—wrapped in crowded theaters.

Plaster Of Paris

Come into your own;
go into your zone.

Talk to dial tone;
get off the phone.

The world you have known
is gone now that you're grown.

Come into your own;
go into your zone.

Let go of the unknown.
See, the stars have shone.

Set cast a broken bone.
You are all alone.

Karmic Cruelty

More goodbyes like swatting flies,
catching mice and crushing roaches.
Twisted pass times like destroying
the ant colony by gasoline and fire.
All these things which I have found
have led me to a horrific discovery:
Oh, to salt the slug; to trap the spider;
to cover the tortoise shell with war paint;
to dissect the lizard while it lives—
to pay homage to its offspring.
Oh, sweet suffering and cruelty,
this thing lives inside of me,
rises like smoke from burning leaves
and they've been dead for centuries.
Distorted eyes and blatant lies—
striking matches just for fun,
dim light warping time, not mine,
and it was all for fun.
For all these crimes I am bound
to never let go of my discovery.
Oh, how I found out seven—
there is no god in heaven.
I was just eleven.
That's how long in heaven?
Oh, please, all of creation be
—not what's left inside of me,

not like smoke from burning leaves,
for they've been dead for centuries.
Broken ties with misted eyes,
still it was awful fun,
hurts so good and pain feels fine
—and it is far from done.

Mirror Monster

I looked into the eyes of my reflection,
and at first, they made no connection.
I stood very still and stared long
and deep into perfection;
two minds conjoined
and made but one
correction—
far away but side by side,
then saw a fair selection.

Low And Limerent

The recluse is privy to a base selection of disregard, withdrawn
from sentiment and society for popular opinion. A lowly sloth
left to his own riffraff devices in sordid houses, rifling through
closets, drawers, and cupboards, and old shoe boxes assorted
with ancient correspondence and faded pictures—incidentally,
preserving as a casket, numerous skeletons from an ancient
roach haven, exterminated by insecticidal indifference.

The hermit borrows from old past, something thought to be lost,
and crawls his way through a catacomb of boxes and books
stacked carelessly atop furniture, to a corner chamber where lies
an uncovered mattress on the bare floor.

A moment of silence to reflect on never, and the drone of static
atmosphere makes him shiver in his underwear, fanning the
photograph clipped between his thumb and index finger to catch
and glint the light off of her portrait, and for a moment he's
reminded of poisoned dead rats rotting below the floorboard,
and can smell their memories—and wants to bed her phantom.

So, passes away into her dreams, reflected through her
captured eyes, and in her pupil darkness, he discovers
a lightswitch, and the bulb just then burns out, and its
last flicker of light snaps one last picture—of her
with mirror eyes, that tell of low and limmerant lies.

Can't Rely

Oh, my dear old friends, my cohorts of absolution,
how you have changed—into acceptable yuppies.
Am I being too familiar; are we now enemies?
So warm and safe in your aloft apartments,
looking down from your windows at me, a stranger.
Did we not part as friends? Is existence in danger?
Have we shared only words? Have my transgressions
repulsed your most delicate senses? Is that why you shy
away from truth and why you scoff at brigands and rogues,
and scoundrels such as myself and the salt of the earth?
Have you to destroy me, or convince others to save yourself?
Are we not all the more beautiful in our most basic design?
Are we to stand on ceremony? Is illusionment sublime,
with airs of virtuous indulgence and the word as a dye?
Forever in shame and indignant and why—must
our passionate dreams just lie down and die?

Death Rattles

Alone now, old—now disappear,
let depression have its way with you.

How cold, so bored, and fear
black mold and bones and glue,

stifling your death agony.
Back then, gold—a tear,

an impression makes it clear to you.
Household, so abhorrent, and dear.

A sack cloth hold the stones and hew
the cinder—form footfalls on destiny.

Unknown how, sold—how austere,
let obsession run away with you.

LSD Day

Would, if I could die forever, in-
side her womb. Still, never born
from that maternal—conceived of
tomb—that I should abort such envy
and shut the fetus up in my old room,
behind the door and beneath the loom
of its own eternal shrill—to be unborn.

Elegance

That's the way of the world;
I feel you. So hidden there,
I see you—you are alone.

With the weight of the world,
I hear you. So very unfair,
I taste you—flesh and bone.

Both in existence and denial,
the blood courses through
with style. No more for you,

enough must do.
Loathe distance—in a while,
the flood will reconcile

the whore in you.
I'm like you;
I'm lost too.

If You're There

Still my thoughts so I can breathe long enough to remember
I'm still alive, even though dead to the world and all its
demented inhabitants.

Turn off the lights so I can open my eyes wide enough to see
another one like me, so I'm not all alone with yet another
morbid fascination.

Ease this determination to break the cycle of consolation,
by means of emotional indulgence and self-sacrifice
through fabricated trust.

Let me believe just one moment, that the feeling is real,
and not have to placate suspicion. Allow me this mercy
—for the love of God.

Silence that voice that induces my migraine with the
impossibility of peaceful solutions and the conclusion
of a restful sleep.

Give me just one absolute aside from passing away
into the nothingness I have found, in this tormented
and twisted state.

Tell me a secret not riddled with lies and touch this
perversion of truth with some purity that I might
not be bitter and cold.

Let loose this obsession, this compulsive regression
that I can for once be whole. Allow me this mercy
—so that I may love God.

The Gods Are Unconcerned

When walking away from his garden,
after having eaten the most ripened
fruit from his daily harvest,
a god spat a stream of saliva
full of bacteria and corrosive enzymes,
still in the process of breaking down
his most recent and bountiful banquet,
onto a discarded heap of produce,
and laughed at himself in good spirit,
while trampling over patches of wild-
flowers—thinking, "such a vain digestion."

All The World Lost

All the world I knew, my childhood—believed it through
and through. The new dawn would hold me, and keep me

always in the woods. I tripped upon her roots and fell,
crying, to my knees—her leaves fell for good,

and to comfort me, she danced and kissed the wind
that sang of ancient poetry.

Mother, please tell me—why has he abandoned me?
Mother, oh, please, mother, do not lie—why has God forsaken me?

She would only kiss me through the wind, her whispered
secrets softening.

Oh, white lie—come back to me. All the world then flew.
My life, bereft of seasons I once knew.

The nightmares overcome me, and keep the folly of all good.
I ripped her sapling roots from hell, rising to my feet

—her leaves fell for good and to comfort me, she danced
and kissed the wind that sang of ancient poetry.

Mother, please tell me—why have you betrayed me?
Mother, oh, please, mother, do not lie. Why have you forgotten me?

She will only kiss me through the wind, her tortured
secrets darkening.

Oh, white lie—come back to me.
All the world I knew—my childhood.

Complex

I remember they said, "those who need love the most,
deserve it the least." I thought I knew why; I never
would have guessed the talk was for me.

I almost killed my best friend and then said I'm sorry;
he almost killed me and then asked,
"why did you not stop me?"

I lost one good girl who could have loved me, had she
not only seen the very worst part of me. I saved
myself for strangers and now I'm alone;

I was once a child but now I'm all grown. The children
have been fed with night, silk and red.
Now, down to bed.

Chalk it all up to hormones and complex self-destruction,
tonics and meaningless sex. It feels so good to be so sad;
I want to go to her and it's too bad.

I wanted a whore but needed her more; she broke through
a wall then fell through a floor. I'm still here, alone—
still floating here, and when it gets dark I can still see her.

Sometimes I wonder where she might be, or if in the daytime
she can see me. I thought to myself, what does it matter—
everything or nothing and I chose the latter.

I reached out my hand but she wouldn't touch me;
I destroyed us and ours,
and she didn't stop me.

Who Am I Kidding

(Speaking of love even though no one said anything,)
seeing the moon through a gopher hole and sometimes
wishing it could shine a little less brilliant, or at least
reel forward, so I can count the holes I shoot through
the sky on a typically lonely night when I decide to
pour my emptiness into all my old long drunk
whiskey bottles and throw them at a man I'd have
become instead of a boy shooting his BB pistol
from his hip.

Nevermind, he can sure shoot but only when he's wasted
in the staying gray time before mine, graying forever
in the ghost town whiskey tavern, where we do what
we do to feel good—for once in awhile, or what about
something like dancing with a woman that I wish I
understood better than a man can.

Then maybe we'd see each other right there in front
of the other and not have to even consider being alone,
another night trying to destroy myself, knowing that I am
and have always been the problem.

Babble

I'm something lower. I'm—over better. I'm taking a header,
I'm—nothing and nowhere, fucking despair—into dark matter.
Something in the blinking lights, time is lost and I do not care.
These endless lines and fallen signs, faster, blaster, caster
—nowhere. Wake up demons; give up dead ends.

Brain explodes into marbles and galaxies form around the gutter.
Clockwise draining in the shower, sup up—black hole ladder.
Climbing into darkness, master gravity, reversing—submerging
splatter. Vain babblings, naked gathering, 'round the fire—burn
together. Hiding lighters, knives, and keys, keeping eyes on lives
and leaves. Why not sleep forever? I will pull the lever.

Anathema

You feel like a nonentity just waiting to discorporate.
Thinking back on things, it's been one hell of a wait.
You tried to be on time and never hesitate, but come
time tomorrow and it's too late. You can never be more
in their mind than—well, who gives a damn about others'
opinions? No point ever telling them, and that is swell.

You came to life with the best of intentions. They can't see
you for the man that you've become; they can only see what
they want to see. You can show them your visions of what's
to come, but they will only see what they want them to be.
They have their religion and their politics, something you
will never understand, but you can adapt to underhanded
deals gone bad and dirty tricks, clever little terms for not
so clever minds, things like war, and things like the times.

You go along with whatever meantime, laughing—crying
 inside, as they paint their lines. And there's nothing you
can do so why the hell do you bother to ever say things like
please or like me too? You know why, it's because they think
you do, and they know—how you do, but they don't know you.

Insecurity

The truth felt nothing like surprise,
another right did wrong kind of song.
I thought I remembered telling lies,
and someone else knew it all along.
In part, it dealt caution to surmise,
yet like a fool you just went along.
Your heart stopped short of its own size,
some fool laughs—some fool dies.

Delusions

Hold—these things you cannot see.
Oh, please—don't drop them,
they are breakable.

Not for show and so, no.
They'll glow when you lose them,
it's so easy, too.

If you've never had a moment,
you won't think twice, you will reach
and you'll miss them.

Renewal

Were the sick ever so real?
Well, I don't know, maybe
God is just another traveler,
bound to catch—cold. Oh, and
if there's a lamp post in the road,
the light will guide you like a sign,
that there's an inn just up ahead.
Have the dead been so fully healed?
Now, I don't know for sure, although,
nature is a wonder, and I do wonder.
Not lost, however, nor alone—or
is it just a shadow there? No, I
can feel it like the sun—falling down,
like the gravity of fate barreling toward.

Things Which Do Not Matter

All these things which do not matter, are all these things that are on the floor; this is not something I can show you —a scattered heap circle the chair, like a Kuiper belt that forms down there, and sometimes you wish someone else could sort them for you. But that's not something you'd ever dare—ask another who is not yet there. So, why can't you just spin the chair in circles?

Every now and then, you dream of what, someone above the ceiling struts? So, you just lean and watch the fan a' spinning—a sensationless motion all around, like some kind of hollow, unearthly ground; and sometimes you hope the room explodes to pieces—all around you.

But it'd just be something else you have to sort through. So, tell it to the space between, or forget and destroy everything, to spin in circles. A mystery globe that sheds its light on everything that once was but now is dusty; that is something else we can't go into—all it ever was or will be, and you feel nothing, like some kind of silence always with you, and it feels you and it wants you. Would that it could ever have another, but it's late at night and you're still searching for the wrong line.

So ask once more by and by, or else go kick the dirt, and spin in circles. It's something you can't have and hold. So, why the hell can't you learn, this is something I cannot get used to? Something always lost will never leave us, like the light turns black once it hits you, and it knows you, and it owns you. Might that figure now be the one—dancing in the dust of earthly squabbles, and to dead music? It was over long before we ever spun our circles.

Best To Have A Friend

Didn't pull the trigger, now we're still not much.
Killed another roach for being one too many.

Thought we knew what for, but never had a clue,
wanted something perfect or just a little better.

Still masturbating dark and light is only laughter.
Boredom creeps in and rarely ever comes up short.

An occasional and momentary panic is something,
even though dull and essentially sensationless.

Sadness—well, boredom is more interesting,
time being an enemy, or so is said.

Best to have a hobby, try keeping from the dead
—life has no fucking meaning anymore.

Regret

Watch the curtains fall forever;
never block the light from dark.
You'll never see these channels
like crosses and fixed positions.
Anger dance the flipping of a coin
—like a mossy oak, and it swamps
the woods with meaning.

To strike the head of a match with deaf
and hollow spaces, sanding the surface
of time with a swarm of flies.
Spackle the sky with clairvoyant glimmer,
and let yourself be sewn into the seem
of things as if they were seen through
her eyes and pretend for a moment
—that it matters.

Personal History

One extreme, or
another.
Highs and lows
define a man.
Shipwrecked vessels,
like stapled landmarks,
crosses staked
into the sand.
No wonders here
on these downhill steps.
To take no comfort
or give no damn.
There is no mystery;
there is no plan.

This Thing Is Understanding

An empty bottle is the only plan.
Is it really a bottle; or just in relation
between table, spirits and hand/eye
coordination and swollen gland?
Where is the cork; and why is the glass
(Is it really a glass, or more proliferation?)
smashed in the sink and what is the trash
doing on the floor, and who is so crass?
But beside the point one is juxtaposed.
It's really a matter of superfluous cessation:
One is almighty, and two Is supposed;
one is recited, and the other composed.

Freeform

We are talking across eternity.
We are running avatar ghosts of
ourselves over the hill.
The hurdle is a little boy's;
he must grow bigger.
The will has no memory;
the whole has no form.

Mayday

I am nothing and no one.
I'm a nothing dance on
zenith and fall on nadir.
I'm a collegiate neptune
wondering under radar.
I am something other/or;
I am something done for.

Vulnerable

In growing up, childhood becomes
an irrelevant secret, which is forgotten
only as much as it is embellished.
We have contrived not only its outcome
but also its meaning.
Our former selves are wasted on us,
and the only ones who know are too little
to comprehend the danger of our denial,
or the shame in their innocence.

Routine Digression

Each new discovery
confirms disappointment.
Forgetfulness lasts
as long as a sleep cycle,
during which time,
a haunting occurs.
Waking is akin to prognosis,
to open the eyes and suddenly
realize the full condition,
even in a dark room.
Still, to already know.
Counter this with apathetic
movement; float out of bed
in a series of rhythmless gestures,
and untimed coordination.
Find a way to the lamp
and turn myself on
for a night, or a day
—a lifetime.

Hair Trigger

Just what is it all about? Oh, like you don't know.
How very well—we both know. So, just what are we to do?
That, I think you already know. No. How long must we
draw this out? No. We've seen this coming.
I need more time—no more time.
Just wait until tomorrow—no longer.
But what about the mind? What about the mind?
What compels us? Mind. Why this quark, this foible?
Quit stalling, quick it comes calling—but if not for the calling.
Must we induce; why—oh, why must we recluse?
Fool, have we not yet died a thousand times more over, when
the floods of our passion were reduced to seasonal drought?
Have we not long foreseen? Do we not have it coming?
Oh, I—just. Oh, nothing. What do we have here?
Oh, just a little something. Old man, hold out your hand.
We, too, both admire brass. Oh, alas—no longer pass.

Bummer

No one gives a damn;
nothing matters—I am.
I feel so far away.
Something has to give,
I can't take this—I can.
I cannot forgive,
everything and nothing.
All has been taken,
taken far away.

Note

To my kith and kin,
who bode me well,
regardless of my sin.
Having heard the knell,
knew I'd never win,
and became a shell
in a sea of gin.
Laughing as I fell
in a heedless glen,
gelded by the bell
—branded by ten.
Existence is hell,
for all or some men.
A barrel or a well,
mind I fall in.

Depression

In a word, if ever there were such a word, so thrown around
as that—the one in which I speak of in retrospect, or more so
even—I doubt, as that well known term which has defined an
entire nation of cultures, to describe my mood, disposition, or
temperamental philosophy—then let us give utterance unto
this expression or figure of speech, as if it were only just
now conceived through instant text messaging, or vague
and passive communication while on the go, twittering
correspondence—the whole experience of human
existence at one's convenience.

If only I may keep that one's attention, long enough so as
to clarify, or maybe even broaden the scope of conversation
and impart upon this collective torpor—a sleight, although
essential endowment in the makeup of an authentic being.
An intellectual reparation of intrinsic value, which has been
degraded to a perverse degree by retribution, insomuch that
the individual will has been completely intoxicated by
grandeur and silenced with gross ramifications.

That said axiom, has become from fallacy to utmost folly
and our most detrimental compromise—that cold, insincere
commonplace, which idealizes capitulation and does not
so much as recognize an obvious adverse effect, without
a designer label of antisocial and psychotic behavioral

disorders, reserved for only the already condemned
and marketed as a fear tactic for memory, such as
the gallows have never preserved—but has instilled
every reservoir of human sentience with a cognisance
devoid of compassion and truth and has turned even
the most profound feeling of emotion—into an inadequacy.

When I'm Dying

Crocodiles and bad kids are sure to live, and
sure to give their tears away for impudence.
It's interesting and calculated. It's fair, it's love,
it's indiscriminate. For all you try, your meddling
can't interrupt that which is always spinning. And
I say, I think you know that luck is disgusting. It's
there, it's love, it's entertaining. Let it move, let it
lose—it's turning us into what we've always had to
be. And that we've seen, and that we're mean—and
that, to be so keen on seeming. Like we're elsewhere
and so different, like it's more than being alive and
human, like it's all just filler and stupid morality, and
it's eternal interfering. You could have been in-
between; you could have seen everything. You could
have been anything. You could have said—not for
nothing, but instead, it all got wasted. You should have
been in the scene; you should have seen a good thing.
You should have been anything. You should have done
something, but instead just laid there dying. And I say
it's fair, it's love, it's disappointing. And I say, it's fair;
I'm there. I'm participating—I'm wasted.

Sadnesses

No one come close, keeping distance
—can't stay clean.

No words, black birds—suddenly
I'm not me.

So there's color I can't see, so I'm
blind—why must I dream?

Summer leaving, such long nights
you'd not believe.

Into something else this season,
out of things—in the seams.

All my thoughts borrow a vision,
all my life and over all.

Satellite Sunlight

Here in this gloom, I'm no fun,
and all alone with what is done.
There's my window—outside the sun,
here in my room where I'm undone.
At night, I seldom feel the sun,
when even it shone, I still felt none.
Outside my window, where the moon won,
a cloud is passing over this sad one.

The Real Me

It's my room but not my house, my clothes but not my life, that I set fire to in youth. Now, I wear my clothes to tatters. I want to burn the house, but it isn't mine to do so. So I destroy all of my letters, but only the ones that I've received. I cannot destroy the ones I've composed because they were sent years ago. But I can reconnect with old contacts and destroy their memory of me, and that is precisely what I have done—disemboweled memories. That's how I am, though; I can't just admit defeat. I have to go the long way around to every place I've ever been. I can't just hang myself or commit seppuku, but I also have to damn myself to hell. Defamation is the only form of affection I have ever known and so I evict myself. I remove myself from every background and welcome no one into the nothing that is the only thing of my own. And this much I am not willing to share. I'm mad, I hate myself and others; I'm sad—they've thrown away my letters. And I've said so much out of anger and bleak despair that no one, not even I, could ever accurately discern the truth of my disparaging, lonesome character, my harrowing —loathsome character.

Lost Face

Being rolled and turned over on this cruel and toxic wave
—to be washed up on that desolate beach, where sea vultures
rejoice as nature's spoiled successors in childlike entitlement.

Bothering no longer these days to flop around, in hopes of being
returned to the depths, where we swam in school of calming
motion, but floating still and cold with nameless dead.

Those whose sacramental vouchers had been declined by nature's
vested and tuxedoed vendors on checkerboard dreamscapes,
(graves and beds staved off by meds.)

I need more room to pace; I hate my own face. There's nothing
better than some different place. Goddamn a wall and all that falls
from grace; goddamn it all, I hate this fucking place.

Now, Then

There was never nearly enough life left
to breathe, let alone to live for a day.
There was hardly a prayer, no matter
the situation or circumstance, there was
also an obstacle. Well, maybe obstacle
isn't the right word. How about—barrier,
partition, divide—chasm? Nary a way
to describe such a frustration, as having
been birthed into a world that was not
accepting any new members from the
womb of a mother that could not assure
herself, even with children. Fathered by
uncertainty and ignorance—to despair
from aspiration for all of life.

Corpses And Dinners

That want, too, will hurt.
A prognosis posthumously delivered
to all that is in between
—futile and vain.
Mortal idiots
needing daggers,
feeding despair.
Generation again,
die, then born again.
Life, not for beginners.
Death, a corpse of winners.

The Miscarriage That Is My Life

Could life have been anything but this,
not mine but yours perhaps—some other,
some different baby, such that is not
a child but a man or even a woman,
but a thing so strange to the world as I?
If so, could it then be within my own
existing—my own, but without insisting,
that my life be dreamt and missed alone?
That being as I am, have not but to die,
nor less the occasion to ask of you why.
Or would that a life could be—not just one,
insist that the heavens give up all but that
one—sun to rise on a world, thus, so alien?
So lacking in recognizable origin or form
that nothing so unique should be allowed,
more or less, than that which is all alone.
Not yours but mine alone, no other,
no beautiful lady that I love or not.
That having no children, I have not but to die,
nor less the desire to ask of them why.

Whatever

They don't know I'm an artist;
that's only because I'm a poet.
So what if I should pass away
undiscovered? Unidentified
lives lost to mundanity,
identities undeserved
—humanity.
Preserve us, saints and sinners;
cast us out among the winners.
Behold, sing for your supper.
Consoled: a downer; an upper.
So frightened and reserved,
just ask the unperturbed.
They'll let you take home leftovers
in belching tupperware.

Strange Bird

I was born into a world of not enough
and raised in a world of too much.
I was allowed to eat until I was fat
but starved of affection and ignored,
(only mocked once in a while by the bored.)
And you'd swear you had died and immediately
were reborn as a buzzard and began pecking
at the dead flesh of your former incarnation.
You'd swear out loud but would not be heard
but shooed away by someone—you shot a bird.
And flew away from someone who shot a bird.

The Cold Is Warm

The cold is warm,
turned dead inside—no form.
Felt sad and died from norm,
a sighed relief or storm.
The cold is warm,
undead beside unborn,
and knelt and lied as sworn
—confide, a thief to mourn.
The cold is warm,
instead inside life formed.
Dealt as one side shorn,
and died as soon as born.
That's why the cold is warm.

Beyond Origin

I live in the place where I grew up.
There—where I felt no connection,
to where I was tagging along.
Further, I have no future to relive the past,
but wait to see what horrors swim
the wake of mundanity.
And get to make a—same decision,
(that is only reminiscent of choice.)
Every day, in endless giving away,
whether or not to lease a bond
with alike or other nameless yond,
(these hideous creatures born from vanity.)

The Only Thing Worse Than Poetry

If I could craft even the most articulate prose, no matter
how eloquent, no matter how bombastic—or sincere
my words, you'd still not understand.

So why write or read for even that matter—Why else?
I need to feel understood, if even only by my future self,
who hates himself more than I have ever hated him.

It's so much more than words; a language can never feel
itself. It can only be used to feel and to make others feel
—but what I've felt is likely not even real.

Not a fiction can testify to its propensity for sadness;
no fantasy can satisfy its bedraggled and misogynistic
celibacy, or whatever that word is—misanthropy.

What's more, or even worse, is being here, left to learn
how to express in words what could only be felt by silence.
And can you believe I was once romantic?

These things called ideals, which once seemed fantastic,
stammered their rhetoric while panting, and all along,
the opposition talking over one another

in scholastic phases, never once considered their words
to be anything other than words, not even feelings, and yet,
the only feelings I have left—are now poems.

I Don't Get To Be A Person

So routinely disillusioned—that
letdown has become a climax.
As if it could really have been for,
something else aside from awkward.
Trying to believe your moon cycle brain
could ever allow you to be a person,
when it's only waxing so to wane,
and your only thoughts are of exclusion.
It's so unfair—that I don't care.

Cliche

Remarkable—now I'm really being lazy, (worthy of remark.)
So what can be said? The dreams only become more obscure;
the days go by smoother with melatonin. The nights are long
and without mystery. I don't drink much anymore these days;
I quit smoking only to start again and stop again—the intervals
are getting shorter still. Everything is cancer, especially
hallmark. I avoid sentiment for fear of cliche—rage. I hate
what I've become and responsibility. I don't feel lost though,
just a bit disillusioned. I blame myself for being naive and
foolish. I no longer wish and hope seems forgotten. I don't
know why I write aside from habit, I haven't felt inspired
for some time now. It doesn't really matter though, so look
away. That isn't cynicism speaking, just the truth. I'm still
capable of love, just the little I have—I save for a select
few, and still it's scarce. I feel old and pointlessness is on
the verge of developing a whole new meaning. My visions
are wasted on me, and it's sad, because I know I'm capable
of so much more. I feel God is toying with me more than
ever—but that's probably just another ego thing, another
tropey thing. I missed being a kid and not another statistic;
I missed a lot of things and lost a lot, too.

Make Your Bed And Lie In It

Being destructive, alright I get it.
But breaking something irreplaceable,
now you have to live without it.
It's hard to do at first, but it gets easier.
Well, maybe not. Maybe it's just convenient,
the more you have to sleep—to feel it.

The Very Same

If day and night are one, we've not seen the same sun.
It may be you and I aren't one, and we've not seen the same sun.
The days of whiskey and weed have turned to nights of anxiety.
To suffer rotgut in constant need.

No humanity. Oh, sobriety.

If day and light have won, we've not seen the same sun.
It may be you and I are one, and we've seen the very same one.
Mother's breast milk that is to feed, has turned to flights inside
of me. To suffer not but in constant need.

No humanity. Oh, sobriety.

If night and light are not one, we've seen the very same sun.
It may be we've all but won, and we've seen the very same one.

Anomie

What a spoiler, what a side—introverted clyde.
Up to nothing, down with—into burning mine.
So postpone some dumb thing. Toss that; cast
aside, someone mumbling, bumbling. Call it
suicide. Differ much too greatly; suffer in disguise.
How anomic, why hide? Extraversion cried, "oh,
for nothing, does it not—feel like an out—inside?"

www.ingramcontent.com/pod-product-compliance
Lightning Source LLC
Chambersburg PA
CBHW070914160726
48004CB00003B/1364